All About Me

Me

By Margaret Clyne

CELEBRATION PRESS
Pearson Learning Group

Contents

What You Need

- construction paper
- a hole puncher
- ribbon
- pencils
- crayons
- markers
- scissors
- glue
- stickers
- photographs

Make a book that's all about you!
Write and draw things you like. Add stickers
and photographs, too. Use the ideas inside
or add your own. Fill as many pages as you
need to make your book.

Get Started

First, choose two sheets of construction paper. Punch holes down the left side of each sheet. These will be the covers of your book.

Write the title of your book on the front cover. Next, add the author's name. That's you! Decorate the cover any way you like.

Write About Yourself

All About Me

I was born on August 28, 1995.

I have long hair and brown eyes.

I'm 3 feet tall.

Damask Talary-Brown

Important Tip
Punch the holes in the paper before you begin writing. Try to punch the holes in the same place on all the sheets of paper.

Now make a page about yourself.
Take a new sheet of paper. Write your name.
How tall are you? What do you look like?
Add a picture of yourself, too.

6

My Life

Ideas

- your best friends' names
- things you do for fun
- instruments you play
- sports you play
- games you like to play

My best friend is Eleni.

I like playing the drums.

Now that you have written about yourself, turn the page over and tell about your life. Do you have a hobby? Do you play sports? Write about how you like to spend your time.

My Favorite Things

I like red.

I like painting.

Ideas
- favorite color
- favorite game
- favorite book
- favorite foods
- favorite animal
- favorite places

I like swimming.

Next, add a page to tell about your favorite things. You can write about things you don't like, too. Don't forget to decorate your page.

Special Things

I wish I could fly.

I want to travel around the world one day.

Being by the sea makes me happy.

Ideas

- what you want to be when you grow up
- how you would change the world
- crazy dreams you've had
- what makes you happy and sad

What are your dreams for yourself?
If you had three wishes, what would they be?
What other special thoughts do you have?
Write about them on the back of the page.

9

Make a Timeline

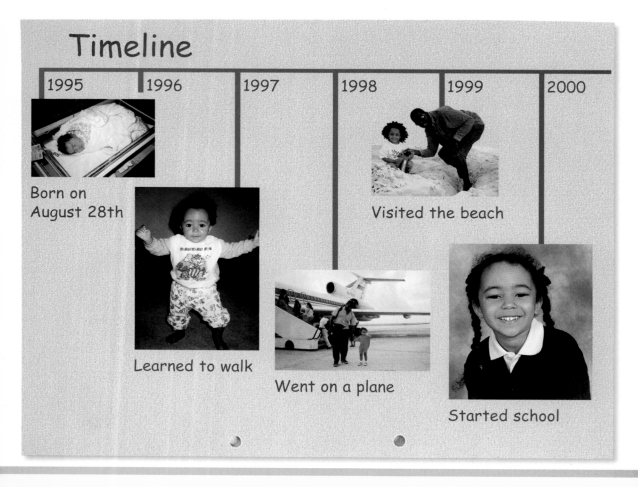

Timeline

| 1995 | 1996 | 1997 | 1998 | 1999 | 2000 |

Born on August 28th

Learned to walk

Visited the beach

Went on a plane

Started school

Now make a timeline for your book. Turn a sheet of paper sideways. The holes should be at the bottom of the page. Draw a line at the top of the page. Then write down important times in your life.

Ideas

- when you took your first steps
- when you learned something special
- when you went to school
- when you went on a trip

On the timeline write about important things that have happened in your life. Talk with your family about things that you did when you were little. Look at family photographs for ideas. Choose your favorite photographs for your timeline.

11

Write About Your Family

My Family

My dad

My mom

Me

I like having fun
with my mom and dad.

Ideas
- family trips
- five things you like about someone
  in your family
- special things people do and say
- your family tree

On the next page of your book, write about
your family members. Write their names and
add drawings of them. Write about things you
like to do together, too.

My Pet

I like giraffes.

I would like to have a horse.

Do you have an interesting pet? Do you want one someday? What do you like about your pet? Maybe your pet deserves its own page!

Write About Your Neighborhood

In this part of your book, tell about where you live. What is your neighborhood like?
Draw a map of your neighborhood.
Show special places, like parks and stores.

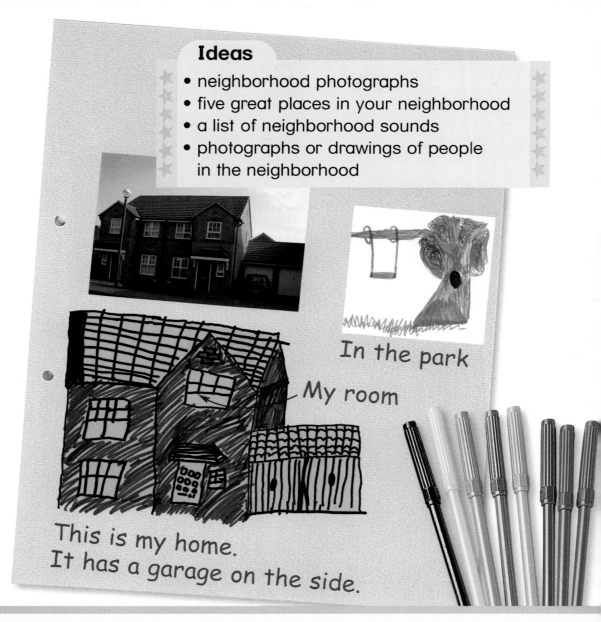

Ideas
- neighborhood photographs
- five great places in your neighborhood
- a list of neighborhood sounds
- photographs or drawings of people in the neighborhood

In the park

My room

This is my home.
It has a garage on the side.

Next, draw your home. You can draw your school, too. Or take photographs of things in your neighborhood. Then paste them onto the page.

Put It All Together

Important Tip
When you put the pages together, keep the punched holes on the left side.

The last step is putting your book together. First, put all the pages in order. Then add the covers. Finally, tie the book together with ribbon. Now you can share your book.